First published in Great Britain by
Pendulum Gallery Press
56 Ackender Road, Alton, Hants GU34 1JS

© TONI GOFFE 1994

IS THERE A LIFE LEFT FOR GRANDPARENTS?
ISBN 0-948912-25-X

PRINTED IN GREAT BRITAIN BY
UNWIN BROTHERS LTD, OLD WOKING, SURREY

DON'T YOU THINK I'M WONDERFUL, FATHERING THE FATHER OF THIS WONDERFUL GRANDCHILD...?

IF I SAY EVERYTHING IS UNDER CONTROL, THEN EVERYTHING IS UNDER CONTROL!

" IT'S ALWAYS THE SAME, WHEN IT'S BEDTIME, YOU CAN NEVER FIND HIM ... "

A PINT OF BITTER, A WHITE WINE AND COULD YOU WARM THIS UP TO 98·4 DEGREES PLEASE...

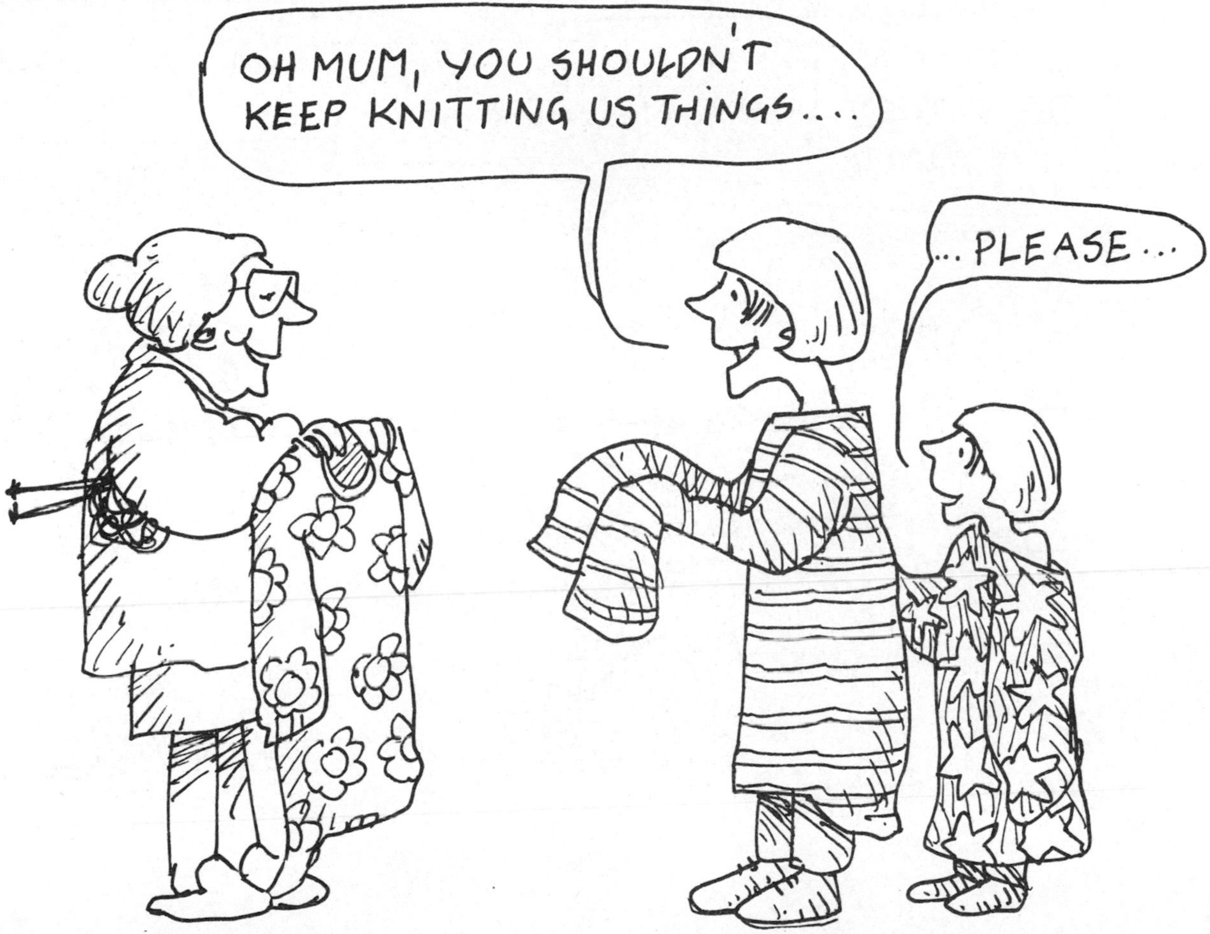
OH MUM, YOU SHOULDN'T KEEP KNITTING US THINGS....
... PLEASE ...

WELL, IF I'M THE ONLY ONE THAT CAN WORK THE VIDEO, I THINK I SHOULD CHOOSE WHAT WE WATCH!

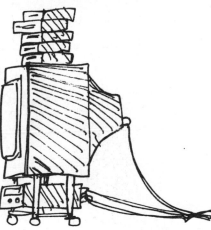

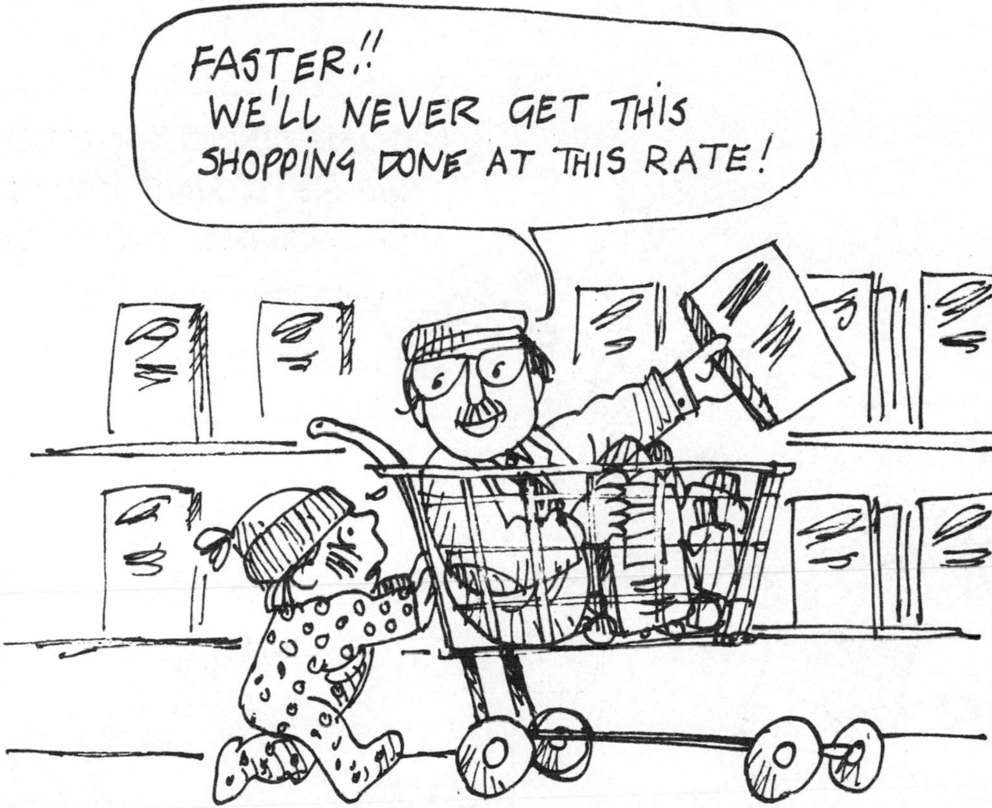
FASTER!!
WE'LL NEVER GET THIS SHOPPING DONE AT THIS RATE!

WELL, THAT'S WHAT HE WANTED FOR HIS BIRTHDAY — SO THAT'S WHAT WE GOT HIM...
CONDOMS